For my daughter, Logan, and for all the little girls who unapologetically follow their dreams.

- Alison Haenlin

www.riselittlequeen.com

This is Kate.

Kate is seven but almost eight.

She loves pizza,

her dog,

and her mom's red sports car.

She loves to fish with her brother and dad on the lake.

But Kate's favourite thing to do is...
skate, skate, skate!

One day Kate declared,
"I want to play on the hockey team!"

"I want to shoot, pass and score... that's my dream!"

So Kate got to work and practiced every day and night.

"But I am the only girl," worried Kate, "what will they think?"

Kate smiled, "Well here goes nothing. One...two...three!"

She zoomed around the ice and made the pucks fly!

Kate couldn't stop smiling
and it was easy to see why.

She made new friends and even scored a hat trick!

While a young boy watched
and copied her with his mini stick.

Kate shot the puck one last time with force then turned a perfect curl.

"Wow!" said the little boy,
"I want to play hockey and skate like a girl!"

SKATE LIKE A GIRL
Text copyright © 2022 by Alison Haenlin
Illustrations copyright © 2022 by Seema Haider

All rights reserved. No part of this publication may be produced, distributed or, transmitted in any form or by any means, including photocopying, recording, or other electronic or mechanical methods, without prior written permission of the publisher, except in the case of brief quotations embodied in critical reviews and certain other non-commercial uses permitted by copyright law

ISBN 978-1-7780870-4   (Hardcover)
ISBN 978-1-7780870-1-1 (Paperback)

RISE LITTLE QUEEN, an independent Publishing House for modern times
riselittlequeen.com

CPSIA information can be obtained
at www.ICGtesting.com
Printed in the USA
BVHW090017140422
634024BV00003B/86